The Price of Freedom:

The Silent Sacrifices of Our Heroes

Thank you to all the have served and allowed me to share their story through my poems.

With Love and Light,
Believe Lylyianne CHt.

Trigger Warning and Legal

Copyright & Trigger Warning

The Price of Freedom: The Silent Sacrifices of Our Heroes
ISBN: 9798339881520
Believe Lylyianne CHt
Mobile, AL 36605
I can be contacted at **BelieveLylyianne@gmail.com**
Or at https://www.Believe.Guru

Trigger Warning: This book may contain subjects and themes that could be triggering for some readers. The experiences and stories shared within, especially regarding trauma, mental health, and healing, are deeply personal and are shared for informational purposes only. Any medical or mental health experiences described are not intended to diagnose, treat, or replace the advice of a licensed medical professional or mental health expert. If you are struggling, please seek the guidance of a qualified professional. If there is subject matter you don't like, don't approve of, is against your belief system, you find offensive. Then Don't read it. I have no Liability over what you do with your free will. If you are having mental issues, call 911. If you need help call me or a therapist.

About the Author

Believe Lylyianne: Master Manifester, Medical Intuitive, and Quantum Healer

Believe Lylyianne is an internationally renowned speaker, published author, and expert in the fields of manifestation and quantum healing. As a medical intuitive and psychic seer, she is dedicated to helping people live their best lives, guaranteeing her work with an unwavering commitment to her clients' success.

Raised by a Marine, Believe has always held a deep connection to the military community. Throughout her 40-year career as a life coach and hypnotherapist, she has treated PTSD and helped countless veterans adjust to life after returning home. She has never turned anyone away, offering Angel sessions at no cost to those in need, funded by her and through generous donations from others.

Believe's expertise extends to reversing lupus, dementia, and other auto-immune diseases, shattering money blocks, saving failing relationships, and manifesting desired lives. Her unique approach blends mastery in quantum energy with intuitive abilities, facilitating both spiritual and physical awakenings for her clients.

If you are ready to transform your life, don't wait. Begin your journey towards lasting change and extraordinary living today. Visit her website at www.Believe.guru. Or BelieveLylyianne.com

Preamble

We the People of the United States, in Order to form a more perfect Union, establish Justice, ensure domestic Tranquility, provide for the common defense, promote the general Welfare, and secure the Blessings of Liberty to ourselves and our Posterity, do ordain and establish this Constitution for the United States of America.

Other Books You May
Find Helpful While Healing

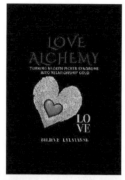

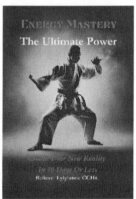

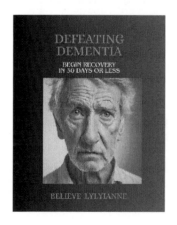

Contents

The Constitution's Song

We the People, bold and free,
In pursuit of unity,
Form a more perfect land of grace,
Justice in its rightful place.

Tranquility we seek to find,
With common welfare for mankind.
Defense of all, both far and near,
Our liberty we hold so dear.

Establish rights, forever bound,
With freedom's echoes all around.
This Constitution, we declare,
For the United States, beyond compare.

Article One, the Congress strong,
Two houses where the laws belong.
Senators, Representatives too,
With power vested, just and true.

Article Two, the President leads,
With duties, honor, mighty deeds.
Commander of the nation's force,
To keep the country's steady course.

Article Three, the judges stand,
With justice weighing in their hand.
Supreme and fair, their eyes on right,
To keep our liberties in sight.
Article Four speaks of the states,
And how their union never breaks.
Each one treated just the same,
Bound in peace, by law and name.

Article Five, to change and grow,
Amendments added, swift or slow.
With future voices heard and strong,
To right what might one day go wrong.

Article Six, the law supreme,
The Constitution reigns the dream.
No higher power shall there be,
Oath of office to keep us free.

Article Seven, the birth is done,
With ratification, we've begun.
Nine states stand, a nation's seed,
Now united, hearts agreed.

Through every age, this charter stands,
A beacon bright in freedom's hands.
The People's voice, in every tone,
The Constitution, carved in stone.

The Silent Watch at Midnight

In the hush of the desert, under starlit skies,
A Marine walks softly, where the silence lies.
His boots trace the sands of an ancient land,
Through abandoned cities, he makes his stand.

No echoes of life in the streets long gone,
Just shadows and whispers of battles drawn.
He guards in the night, where the world sleeps still,
A lone sentinel with an iron will.

His rifle rests easy, cradled with care,
Eyes sharp as the wind moves through the air.
He walks for his family, he walks for the flag,
Each step a promise, never to lag.

He knows the peace is fragile, thin,
And he is the line that holds it in.
The weight of duty on his back,
In the midnight hour, there's no turning back.

He doesn't ask for praise or cheers,
Just to serve, to calm the fears.
For those he loves and calls his own,
He guards the ground, but feels alone.

Yet in his heart, a fire burns bright,
The will to protect through darkest night.
In cities lost and deserts wide,
A Marine stands tall with honor and pride.

So, as the world rests in peaceful sleep,
He takes the silent watch, his vow to keep.
In the stillness, he stands, both strong and true,
Guarding the dream of red, white, and blue.

Footsteps Echoing in a Distant Land

I hear you, soldier, in the early dawn,
Your footsteps soft, yet heavy
with the weight of all you carry
Not just the gear, not just the rifle
strapped firm to your side,
But the burden of a nation's hope,
the prayers of those you leave behind.

Far from the quiet streets
where you were born,
Where the flag waves gently,
unnoticed in the breeze,
Now you walk where the wind cuts harsh,
Where the sands are cruel,
and the cities echo with the ghosts of war.

Your heartbeat aligns
with the pulse of this distant land,
Each step a whisper in the soil

A promise kept, though the miles
 stretch long and the nights grow cold.
And still, you march, with steadfast resolve,
Through the heat and the dust, through the
unknown.

I see you, warrior, under the same sun
that rises over home,
Yet here, it feels distant alien, indifferent.
But in your chest beats the rhythm of America's
heart,

Your every breath is a tribute to the freedom you
defend.
Ah, what thoughts fill your mind
as you tread this foreign earth?
Do you recall the faces of loved ones
The touch of your mother's hand,
the laughter of your child?
Does their memory warm you
when the chill of battle seeps deep into your bones?

O soldier, I sing for you,
You who stand where others dare not tread,
In places that will never know your name,
But forever bear the imprint of your passage
The silent testimony of those who serve, and
sacrifice, and love In ways too deep for words.

Let the echo of your footsteps carry through the
valleys,
Across the oceans, through the fields of home,
So that those who sleep in peaceful beds
Might stir in quiet gratitude,
Unaware that it is your shadow that guards their
dreams.

O distant land, you hold our finest sons,
Our daughters brave and true Hold them gently,
And may their footsteps always find the way back,
Through the storms, through the struggle,
Back to the soil of their birth,
To the arms that long for their return.

For even as they march, far from home and hearth,
Their hearts beat here, among us
Footsteps echoing, forever, in this land of the free.

The Last Kiss Before Deployment

It lingers, soft and bittersweet,
That last kiss before you leave.
A fleeting touch, a gentle breath,
A silent promise underneath.

Your eyes, they speak the words unsaid,
A thousand fears, a thousand prayers.
In this moment, time stands still,
As I held on, unprepared.

The world outside is moving fast,
But here, in this small, sacred space,
We wrap ourselves in fragile love,
Our hearts entwined in one embrace.

Your hand, it trembles as you pull away,
Yet I feel the strength within your grasp.
You walk with duty in your veins,
Though in my soul, I wish you'd stay.

I kiss you like it's all we have,
Like time might let us cheat its grasp.
One kiss to carry through the storm,
To hold you close when you're too far.

And when the skies are filled with fire,
And the nights grow long and cold,
I'll think of this our last goodbye,
And hold it tight, more precious than gold.

For though you go to serve the land,
To guard and fight, to keep us free,
That kiss will live in every breath,
A part of you, still here with me.

So, go, my love, with courage bold,
And know that through the miles and time,
That last kiss will remain with us,
Until your lips return to mine.

Letters from Home, Stained with Tears

The paper crinkles in your hands,
Fingers tracing lines of ink,
Words that traveled oceans wide,
From a place where hearts still sink.

Each sentence whispers through the air,
Like voices caught between the miles
Telling stories of a world unchanged,
Yet missing you through all the while.

The lines are smudged, the edges worn,
For every night, I've held them tight.
The ink has bled where tears have fallen,
Silent marks of love and fright.

I write to you with shaking hands,
Unsure of what is safe to say.
Do I tell you of the quiet here,
Or how I break each passing day?

I speak of children growing fast,
Of laughter you should be here to hear.
But in the spaces, the truth seeps out,
These letters soaked with silent fear.

I try to smile through every line,
To send you strength across the sea.
But every word is heavy now,
With all the things I cannot be.

I wish my tears could reach your cheek,
A touch of home to ease the ache.
For though you're strong, my love, my heart,
I fear the weight you cannot shake.

So, take these letters, stained with tears,
And know they carry more than pain.
They hold my love, my hope, my faith,
A promise that we'll meet again.

And when the day comes, you return,
These pages will be dry and clear.
For every tear I've shed, my love,
Will vanish when you're finally near.

A Folded Flag Draped in Love and Loss

O sacred cloth, folded tight in trembling hands,
You who once soared high above, kissed by wind
and sun,
Now rest in silence heavy with meaning,
A symbol of life, of duty, of love eternal.

I see you, draped in solemn honor,
Resting upon the stillness of one who gave all
O fallen soul, brave and true,
This flag, now folded, speaks your name in every
thread.

O! How the stars still shine, though dimmed by the
weight of tears,
And the red stripes bleed, not of dye, but of
sacrifice,
The white, pure as the hearts left behind
The mothers, the fathers, the children, the lovers.

Here, beneath the stretch of sky,
In the quiet hum of gathered breath,
We hold this cloth, this folded testament,
And with it, the story of a life lived for something
greater.

O soldier, your heart beats in the folds of this flag,
Your love, your laughter, your whispered dreams
Though now hushed, they sing in the wind that
carries this banner high,
And in the hands that clasp it close, cradled in grief
and pride.

I feel your presence here, woven into the fabric of
this land,
Each stitch a step you took, each star a dream you
held.
Your loss, a heavy stone in our chests, yet a light
that guides us still.
You have not gone but risen into the heart of this
nation.

O flag! O folded tribute, you are not mere cloth,
But the very pulse of those who serve and fall,
Draped in the arms of those who loved and lost,
Yet never forget the cost of freedom etched in every
crease.

Take this flag, you who mourn,
Hold it close, for it carries the spirit of the brave,
The ones who walked into the fire so that we might
rest in peace,
Their legacy, forever wrapped in the red, white, and
blue.

O America, remember the souls beneath the stars,
The hands that held you in life, and now in death
This folded flag, heavy with love and loss,
A reminder that freedom is borne from sacrifice,
And draped in the undying love of the fallen.

A Child's Wish for One More Bedtime Story

The moon peeks softly through the blinds,
Its silver light a quiet glow,
But tonight, the chair beside the bed
Is empty, where you used to go.

No sturdy hands to turn the page,
No voice to chase the fears away.
You promised, Dad, to come back soon,
But now you're gone, so far away.

The siren calls took you that night,
A hero dressed in blue so proud,
You left to keep the streets at peace,
To shield us from a world so loud.

But here, within these four safe walls,
I wait and wish for you once more
For one more tale before I sleep,
One last adventure to explore.

I close my eyes and see you there,
The storybook held in your hands,
You'd read of knights and dragons fierce,
Of far-off lands and golden sands.

But now the pages lie untouched,
The stories frozen in their place,
I wish for just one bedtime tale,
And one more glimpse of your kind face.

They say you're a hero, brave and true,
You kept the city safe that day.
But I would trade the cheers and flags
To have you here, not far away.

Just one more night, just one more tale,
Just one more hug before I sleep.
I miss you, Dad, and in my dreams,
Your stories in my heart I keep.

So, though you're gone, I still pretend,
And hold the book the way you would.
I wish for one more bedtime tale,
To feel once more your love so good.

The Strength of the One Who Stays Behind

It's not just the soldier who stands in the line,
Not just the one who wears the boots,
Who salutes the flag and marches on
No, it's the family that joins the fight too.

For when the soldier boards the plane,
The heart of the home is never the same.
The spouse, the child, the parents too,
Are soldiers now, in all they do.

The strength of the one who stays behind
Is forged in moments small and kind
In holding the fort when the winds blow hard,
In wiping the tears that come unbarred.

They don't wear medals, they don't wear stripes,
But their battles are fought through sleepless
nights.
Their heart goes with every step you take,
While they hold on, strong, for your sake.

They take on the weight of the day-to-day,
Making sure the kids are okay.
They smile when inside they're torn in two,
For they're fighting this battle right alongside you.

It's setting the table for one less seat,
It's hearing your voice in every heartbeat.
It's waiting in silence, when news doesn't come,
And hoping and praying until the war's won.

It's the bravery that no one sees,
The quiet heroism in keeping the peace.
The strength to stand when the world feels wrong,
The courage to wait, to be steady and strong.

For every soldier that goes to fight,
A family waits through the endless night.
And though they may not march in the sand,
Their hearts beat with you, hand in hand.

So, here's to the ones who stay behind,
The silent warriors of a different kind.
For it's not just one who answers the call
It's the strength of a family that fights through it
all.

Boots Left at the Door, Untouched

The boots sit silent by the door,
Worn and weathered, like before.
They wait in stillness, side by side,
A quiet symbol of duty's pride.

Each morning, they are pulled on tight,
To face the dangers of the night
Through smoke and fire, through fear and pain,
They tread where others would refrain.

The sirens call, the radios hum,
And off they go, no time to run.
First in line when chaos reigns,
To guard the streets, to ease the strain.

But tonight, those boots remain unmoved,
Untouched, unworn, they stand removed.
For though they wait, their keeper's gone,
A hero lost before the dawn.

The door swings shut, but not with ease,
A quiet house, a heart that grieves.
The echoes of their final run
Live in the shadows of what's undone.

The family waits, the house stands still,
While boots rest empty, by their will.
The hands that once laced up those soles
Now serve in memories, deep and whole.

These boots symbols of every call,
Of courage answered, big and small.
They'll stand there waiting, day by day,
For one who's walked another way.

And though they sit, untouched by time,
Their story lives in every climb,
In every blaze and every tear,
In every act that conquered fear.

For first responders leave a mark,
In homes, in hearts, in places dark.
And though the boots may gather dust,
Their legacy remains with us.

The Weight of Duty, Heavy on the Heart

I sing of you, soldier, walking the long road,
Of you, Marine, with eyes sharp, steady under the
blazing sun
And you, sailor, whose soul rides the tides, whose
heart beats with the pulse of distant shores,
I sing of your duty, noble and raw, and of the
burdens you carry unseen.

What weight is this that pulls at your chest, that
lives in your hands, calloused and strong?
What name do you give this heaviness, this silent
anchor upon your spirit?
It is duty shining and relentless, a fire that never
dims
The oath you swore, bound to honor, to country, to
the flag that waves above,
A love so deep it stings, and yet you stand,
unmoved, marching forward into the unknown.

O soldier, how the weight presses, yet still you rise!
In your heart beats the thunder of battles yet
fought,

The cries of comrades etched in memory,
the faces of home that float before you
in the night,

And still, you stand your heart burdened, but
unbroken,
Duty your guide, though it bends the spirit and
leaves its mark upon your soul.

I see you, weary yet unshaken,
The ground beneath your feet trembling, the sky
above both vast and small,
Yet your step does not falter.
For what is this weight compared to the love of
country?

What is the ache of duty when weighed against the
freedom it defends?
O soldier, your strength is not in the steel you carry,
Not in the rifle slung upon your back or the armor
you wear,

But in the quiet resolve that fills your heart,
In the moments when fear whispers close, and you
push it aside with the strength of belief
A belief in something larger than yourself, in the
promise of liberty,

A belief that echoes through time, carved in the soil beneath your feet.
And though the weight of duty presses heavy,
Though it pulls at your every breath, I see you stand tall

A pillar of courage, a testament to sacrifice.
For in your heart burns the fire of a nation,
And in your hands rests the hope of a people,
O soldier, who walks with the weight of duty, heavy on the heart,
You carry us all, and we honor you.

The Sound of Freedom in a Soldier's March

Listen close, the footsteps fall,
Echoing through the morning's call.
A steady rhythm, bold and true,
The sound of freedom marching through.

With every step, a promise made,
Of sacrifice that won't be swayed.
Across the fields, through desert sand,
A soldier walks for this great land.

The cadence sharp, the heartbeat strong,
In every stride, where they belong.
The sound of boots upon the earth,
A nation's hope, a people's worth.

It's not the crack of guns that sings,
Nor fighter jets with mighty wings,
But in the march of those who stand,
That freedom rings across the land.

Through cities vast, through forests deep,
Through nights where even stars don't sleep,
A soldier's march is loud and clear,
It speaks of peace, it conquers fear.

So, as you walk, O soldier brave,
With every step, the flag you save.
The sound of freedom in your pace,
A gift you give with silent grace.

We hear it now, in hearts and skies,
In every tear a family cries.
The sound of freedom, strong and sure,
In every soldier's march endures.

The Unbreakable Bond Between Comrades

In the dust and dirt, through fire and rain,
Where bullets fly and skies are stained,
There's a bond that forms, fierce and true
A bond between the many, forged by the few.

It's born in the silence before the fight,
In whispered prayers through the darkest night,
In the glance that says more than words ever could,
In the grip of hands that have understood.

They march together, side by side,
One heart, one mind, through fear they stride.
For when the battle rages wild,
They face it together, neither one exiled.

In every struggle, through every tear,
They find their strength when the end seems near.
No rank or name can tear apart
The bond that beats in every heart.

They carry each other when legs give way,
And hold the line till the break of day.
For in the chaos, in the storm,
It's the unbreakable bond that keeps them warm.

Through every scar, through blood and bone,
They know they never stand alone.
For once you've walked through the flames of war,
You are bound to each other, forevermore.

It's a bond that stretches beyond the fight,
Beyond the day and into the night.
Through peace, through life, it stays the same
A brotherhood, eternal flame.

So, here's to the comrades, near and far,
Whose unbreakable bond is their guiding star.
No force on earth, no time, no space,
Can sever the ties that battles embrace.

The Fire That Rages Inside and Out

The battle's done, the war is past,
They've finally made it home at last.
But peace, it seems, is hard to find,
For there's a war that rages in the mind.

Outside, the world goes on unchanged,
But inside, everything feels rearranged.
The sounds of home, once soft and clear,
Now echoes loud and brings back fear.

The fire that burned in foreign lands
Still smolders here, within their hands.
Though they've laid down their arms and gear,
The flames of war remain so near.

In crowded rooms or silent nights,
The memories come, the distant fights.
The mind, it burns with sights unseen,
The scars of battle sharp and keen.

They smile for loved ones, hold them tight,
But feel the heat of another fight.
For though the war was left behind,
It left its fire deep in the mind.

Yet still they stand, though flames persist,
And fight a battle that can't be missed.
The fire outside may slowly fade,
But the one inside is where they've stayed.

O soldier, brave through land and air,
We see the fire that you bear.
Know that in this world of home,
You do not fight this fire alone.

For every flame that burns your heart,
There are hands to help pull it apart.
Though the fire rages, fierce and wide,
We stand with you, both side by side.

The fire within may never cease,
But together, we will find your peace.
And in that peace, may you find light
A way to quench the endless fight.

"I'm Fine"

"I'm fine," he says with a hollow smile,
As he walks through a world that feels exiled.
Home again, but still far away,
The battles he fought never seem to stray.

"I'm fine," she whispers, eyes cast down,
Trying to hide the weight she's found.
The laughter of children rings in her ears,
But it's drowned by the echoes of distant fears.

They come back home, but the war comes too,
Invisible scars that no one knew.
Their bodies are here, but their minds remain
In the dust, in the fire, in the endless strain.

They sit at the table, a quiet space,
With memories they can't erase.
Their families ask, "Are you okay?"
But the words don't come, so they turn away.

"I'm fine," they say, though the night feels long,
And the strength to hold it all feels gone.
For no one sees the battles inside,
The ghosts they carry, the pain they hide.

They need the help they're too proud to ask,
To break the silence, to drop the mask.
But the world keeps turning, unaware,
Of the heavy burdens they still bear.

In their hearts, the war rages on,
Though the battlefield seems long gone.
And though their bodies may be home,
They fight their battles all alone.

"I'm fine," they say, but it's far from true
There's so much more they're going through.
They need a hand, a voice, a friend,
Someone to help their spirits mend.

So let us listen, let us see
The silent cries for help that be.
For "I'm fine" is just a veil they wear
A call for love, a need for care.

And may we stand, arms open wide,
To help them heal, to be their guide.
For the war they fight is far from done,
And their hardest battles have just begun.

A Mother's Prayer Whispered in the Dark

In the stillness of the midnight hour,
When the world is hushed, and hearts turn sour,
A mother kneels beside her bed,
With heavy thoughts and prayers unsaid.

Her children gone to lands unknown,
Where danger waits, where war has grown.
She lights a candle, soft and low,
And whispers words that only mothers know.

"Bring them home," she breathes with care,
A quiet, urgent, desperate prayer.
"Keep them safe in your embrace,
Guide them through this darkest place."

She prays for strength they'll never see,
For courage in the face of misery.
She prays for peace beneath their feet,
And that their hearts stay pure, complete.

Her hands, they tremble as they fold,
Her whispered plea so soft, so bold:
"Let them see the light of dawn,
Bring them back before too long."

In every tear that slides unseen,
She holds the hope of what could be.
And though the night is cold and wide,
Her faith burns steady, bright inside.

For in her heart, a mother knows
The love that through the darkness grows
A love that reaches 'cross the miles,
To cradle them in quiet smiles.

And so, she prays, though no one hears,
Each word wrapped tight in unspoken fears.
A mother's prayer whispered in the dark,
A silent flame, a steadfast spark.

"Bring them home," she prays again,
"From every storm, from every pain.
Hold them close when I cannot,
Protect the lives they haven't forgot."

And though the night feels long and deep,
She knows her vigil she must keep.
For every breath her children take,
A mother's prayer, she will not break.

Until the day they're home once more,
She'll whisper prayers through every door.
A mother's love, forever strong
A prayer to bring her babies home.

The Flag Waving in the Desert Wind

I sing of the flag, bold and brilliant, waving in the desert wind!
O stars and stripes, how you dance amidst the swirling sands,
Your colors, bright and true, rippling through the heat of the sun,
In a land far from home, where warriors rise, where our sons and daughters stand.

Here, in this vast and barren place,
Where the earth itself seems to tremble beneath the weight of war,
Where the horizon stretches long and empty, yet full of purpose,
Our men and women march, their hearts alight with the fire of liberty.

O! I see them in their steadfast ranks,
Faces turned to the harsh sun, unyielding,
For what is the desert heat compared to the flame of freedom within?
They stand, unbroken, their boots sinking into foreign soil,

Carrying with them the hope of a distant land, the promise of peace.

The flag waves above them, as if to bless each footstep,
A symbol of the cause they carry,
A banner that knows no defeat, that speaks of home—
Home, where the hearts of a nation beat for them,
Home, where mothers whisper prayers in the dark and fathers stand proud.

And here, beneath the blazing sky, beneath the endless expanse,
Our soldiers hold the line
Not for glory, not for gold, but for something greater,
For the belief that freedom is worth every step, every drop of sweat, every tear.
O Desert Storm, where the winds of fate did blow fierce,
Where our men and women faced the tempest and stood tall,
I see them still, in my mind's eye
The dust rising around them, the flag unfurling like a beacon of hope,
Waving high above the battlefield,
A silent sentinel in the desert wind.

The storm rages, but they do not falter,
For in their hearts, the flag waves too
In every breath they take, in every beat of their
weary hearts,
The stars and stripes shine bright.

And as the desert wind howls across the sands,
It carries with it the whispers of home,
The echoes of a grateful people, the songs of
freedom's march.
O flag! O mighty banner! You wave for them all,
For the fallen and the brave, for the ones who
return and the ones who stand still.

In the desert wind, I hear the roar of courage,
The unspoken bond of comrades,
The weight of duty heavy upon their shoulders yet
worn with pride.

And when the storm has passed,
When the dust has settled and the silence comes,
The flag will remain, waving in the desert wind,
A testament to those who took a stand,
To those who fought in the name of freedom,
To those who will never be forgotten.

O stars and stripes! You wave not just in the desert,
But in the hearts of all who believe in what is right,
In the hearts of those who stood, and still stand,
For the light of liberty, burning bright in the desert
wind.

A Hero's Homecoming, Bittersweet

They threw the banners, waved the flags,
Shook his hand and slapped his back.
"Welcome home!" the neighbors cheered,
But life's a bit more weird than they appeared.

For two long years, she held it down,
Ran the ship, never wore a frown.
Bills got paid, the kids stayed fed,
She even learned to fix the shed!

Now, here he is, back in the fold,
With stories of deserts and nights so cold.
But suddenly, things seem quite unclear,
Like when she grabs her keys, he says, "Where you goin', dear?"

"To the store," she says, like it's no big deal,
But he squints like she's plotting some kind of heist or steal.
"The store?" he asks, like it's brand-new news,
As if the milk just falls from the sky when she chooses.

Two years, she thinks, with a smirk on her face,
She's been going to the store without leaving a
trace!
But now, every step, there's a question to bear,
Like, "Did you really buy that? Do we need more
pears?"

She smiles and nods, though she wants to groan,
Because now she's not just living alone.
No more one-woman show, she has her star,
But adjusting's tougher when he asks, "What's in
the jar?"

"That's spaghetti sauce," she says with a grin,
"Remember, we used to eat it way back when?"
And while he's catching up on things at home,
She secretly wishes she could roam.

Not that she's mad, no, that's not the case,
It's just strange to have someone in her space.
The remote's now lost in his new domain,
And he says, "What happened to all the football
games?"

He means well, he does, she knows it's true,
But living alone meant she'd just do.
Now there's a buddy for all her tasks,
Even when all she wants is to relax.

It's the little things those things you forget
Like laundry routines and where shoes should be set.
He's a hero, no doubt, strong and brave,
But who knew "put your socks away" would be the hill she'd save?

So, they laugh through the mess, the quirks, the mix,
Finding new ways, their own little fix.
And as she grabs the keys once more for the store,
She smiles at him waiting by the door.

"Want to come with me?" she says, with a grin,
"Let's make this homecoming a proper win."
He nods and laughs, "I'll give it a try."
Because adjusting to home? Well, it's all both of them, eye to eye.

The Endless Road to Healing

Night falls, and here I am again,
Caught in the darkness, drowning within.
The silence creeps, the shadows grow,
And once again, I'm left to know

The road to healing stretches far,
Like chasing ghosts, like grasping stars.
Each step I take, the ground gives way,
And night terrors rise where dreams should stay.

The clock ticks on, but time stands still,
As fear takes root, against my will.
I fight the urge to scream or cry,
But the weight inside won't let me fly.

A voice calls out, it pulls me back,
Talks me off the edge, away from the crack
The crack in my mind where the terror lies,
The part of me that just wants to die.

They say I'll heal; they say I'll mend,
But this endless road, where does it end?
For every night, I start anew,
Falling deeper, losing view.

The faces haunt, the echoes scream,
And every moment feels like a dream,
A nightmare, twisted, sharp, and cold,
Where even hope can't take a hold.

I want to run, but there's no place,
No haven found in time or space.
Just me and these walls, these endless fears,
The pain of years, the silent tears.

Talk me down, please, once again,
Help me breathe, count to ten.
For night has come, and here I stand,
On the ledge, reaching for a hand.

But even with the hand I take,
This road to healing makes me ache.
It's long, it's cruel, it shows no end
Each night I break, each dawn I bend.

And though the darkness pulls me in,
I'll walk this road, through thick and thin.
For somewhere, somehow, there's light, they say,
And maybe, just maybe, I'll find it someday.

The Medal That Weighs More Than Gold

It glimmers in the sunlight's glow,
A medal worn with pride,
But what it cost to earn that prize
Is carried deep inside.

It weighs more than the finest gold,
More than the world could see
It holds the weight of sacrifice,
Of pain and bravery.

For every shine upon its face,
There's a scar that's never healed,
A memory etched in silence
On a far-off battlefield.

It tells a story, sharp and true,
Of comrades lost and tears,
Of nights spent wide awake in fear,
Of battles fought for years.

The weight of duty, courage born,
Of homes left far behind,
Of lives forever changed by war,
And struggles of the mind.

This medal's weight is not in steel,
Nor ribbon, clasp, or thread
It holds the burden of a heart
That fought while others bled.

It's not just honor that it bears,
But grief and silent pain,
For though it gleams upon the chest,
It comes with heavy strain.

It weighs more than the world can know,
This medal made of loss
Of promises that won't return,
Of sacrifice, the cost.

So, when you see it shine with pride,
Remember what it holds
The soul of every soldier brave,
A medal more than gold.

The Uniform Hanging in the Closet, Waiting

There it hangs, in quiet grace,
A uniform that once knew pace.
The creases sharp, the colors bold,
But now it waits, its stories told.

Once it walked where fear was strong,
Worn by those who marched along.
Through fields of dust and skies of gray,
It bore the weight of night and day.

The battles fought, the wars survived,
The dreams of home kept hope alive.
But now it hangs, a silent guard,
Its fabric soft, its edges scarred.

No more the boots that hit the ground,
No more the orders ringing loud.
The medals earned, the ranks long past,
Now folded neatly, still at last.

The life it lived, the blood it knew,
The friends it lost, the battles too.
And though it hangs in quiet peace,
Its heart is full, its work's release.

For in its threads are memories kept,
Of sleepless nights and tears wept.
Of comrades gone, but not forgot,
Of moments won, of lessons taught.

Now just a shell of what it was,
It waits, without a cause because
The soldier's hands have laid it down,
And only echoes wear its crown.

But still it stands, though battles fade,
A testament to the price once paid.
And there it stays, forever true
The uniform that carried you.

Courage Beneath the Helmet and Vest

Beneath the helmet, beneath the vest,
Beats a heart that never rests.
A heart of courage, strong and true,
In the lives of our boys in blue.

With every call, with every fight,
They stand for justice, day and night.
Through city streets, in the darkest hour,
They face the storm; they hold the power.

But it's not just the badge or gear they wear,
It's the quiet strength that shows they care.
For every moment, they put aside
Their fears, their doubts, their tears inside.

They see the world at its worst and best,
Yet still they stand, without protest.
Through chaos, loss, and pain untold,
They keep their ground, they remain bold.

Beneath the vest, a soul that aches,
For all the hearts the world forsakes.
But still they rise, they press ahead,
For every life they've sworn to defend.

Their courage shines, though few may see
The weight they bear, silently.
It's not in words, but in their deeds,
In every step, where honor leads.

So, when you see them passing by,
Know they carry more than meets the eye.
For beneath the helmet, beneath the vest,
Is a courage that never comes to rest.

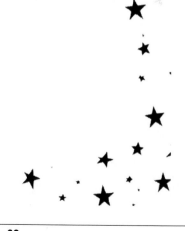

The Radio Crackling with Urgent Voices

The radio crackles, the voices rise,
Urgent calls beneath dark skies.
In a room with screens and static hum,
The operators wait for what may come.

"911, what's your emergency?" they say,
Calm and steady through the fray.
Behind the voices, lives unfold,
Stories of fear, both young and old.

The frantic words, the cries for aid,
The desperate whispers in the shade
Each one a life, a plea, a prayer,
And they are there, always aware.

They stay unseen, behind the wire,
Where every moment's charged with fire.
Their hands move fast, their voices clear,
They push aside their silent fear.

For in the chaos, they are the guide,
The unseen heroes by our side.
They map the streets, the hearts, the pain,
They talk you through the hardest strain.

The radio crackles, the night moves on,
But they hold steady until the dawn.
With every call, they give their best,
Though no one sees them take a rest.

"Help is coming, stay with me,"
They say with calm intensity.
And though they never leave their chair,
Their voices travel everywhere.

So, here's to them, the unseen crew,
Who answers the calls and guide us through.
The radio crackles, but they don't tire—
In every word, they fight the fire.

The Scars No One Sees

The battle's over, the war is done,
But the quiet fight has just begun.
For though they've come back from the fray,
The scars no one sees still stay.

No bandage wraps, no cast in sight,
No medal gleams for this silent fight.
But deep inside, where the darkness lies,
The war still rages behind their eyes.

They smile, they laugh, they play the part,
But echoes linger in the heart.
The sounds of war, the cries, the fears,
Still whisper softly through the years.

The scars no one sees, they tell no tale,
Of sleepless nights or spirits frail.
Of waking to a world that's changed,
Where nothing feels quite rearranged.

They walk among us, heroes still,
But carry burdens, sharp and real.
For though the guns have ceased to fire,
The soul is caught in tangled wire.

And when the world seems calm and clear,
Inside, they battle doubt and fear.
For every step, a weight they bear,
A ghost of war that lingers there.

The scars no one sees, they hide away,
In quiet moments, day by day.
But in their silence, strength remains,
To carry on through unseen pains.

So, look beyond the surface bright,
See the courage in their quiet fight.
For though the scars are hard to find,
They live within, and yet they shine.

A war within, a battle faced,
With bravery that can't be traced.
The scars no one sees, but they're still there,
A testament to all they bear.

The Lullaby of Distant Gunfire

In the stillness of the night, it comes,
A sound that hums beneath the drums,
Of silence thick and stars so far,
A lullaby from fields of war.

The distant crack, the echoed round,
Like whispers carried on the ground.
It hums through valleys, across the plains,
A tune composed in battle's veins.

The lullaby of distant fire
Lulls the soldiers, though they tire.
Their bodies rest, but minds can't sleep,
For in the distance, echoes creep.

Each shot a note, each burst a chord,
That sings of what they can't afford
A dream, a peace, a moment's ease,
For in this song, there's no release.

But still, they lie beneath the sky,
With weary hearts and heavy sighs.
The lullaby of war's refrain
Plays softly in the soldier's brain.

And as the night slips gently by,
They listen close, their nerves awry.
For every pop and every crack
Reminds them what they're holding back.

The world, it sleeps, but they remain
Awake beneath the phantom strain
Of distant gunfire, soft and low
A tune the world will never know.

A lullaby, but not of peace,
A song that brings no sweet release.
For in its rhythm, they still fight,
Long after the fall of night.

The Heart of a Warrior, Softened by Love

In the chaos, in the storm,
Where flames rise high, where lives are torn,
There stands a warrior, brave and true,
With a heart that beats for me and you.

The sirens blare, the danger calls,
Through smoke and ash, through crumbling walls.
Their courage shines, their strength runs deep,
Yet there's a softness they still keep.

For though their hands may fight the fire,
Their heart is fueled by something higher
A love that drives each daring feat,
A tenderness beneath their feet.

The world sees only strength and might,
A warrior in the darkest night.
But behind the badge, behind the shield,
Is a love that never yields.

It's in the way they hold a hand,
Of those who cannot understand.
It's in the words they softly say,
To comfort those lost on their way.

For every act of valor bold,
There's a love that won't grow cold.
A heart that fights, yet still believes
In all the hope that love achieves.

The warrior's soul is fierce and strong,
But love has been there all along.
In every rescue, every save,
It's love that makes them truly brave.

The heart of a warrior, softened by love,
Is the truest strength that rises above.
For in their battle, day and night,
It's love that gives their fight its light.

The Waiting Room Filled with Quiet Hope

The clock ticks slow, the hands move still,
Each second stretched against our will.
The waiting room, both bright and dim,
Where silence speaks and hope grows thin.

Faces drawn, eyes fixed ahead,
In whispered prayers, words left unsaid.
A mother clutches her trembling hand,
A father stands, trying to withstand.

Each breath a fragile, fleeting thing,
As quiet hope begins to cling.
To every sigh, to every glance,
To every whispered, desperate chance.

The room is full, yet feels so small,
As time seems frozen, trapped in thrall.
But somewhere, hope is softly spun,
A fragile thread from which we're hung.

In each soft shuffle of a chair,
In every heartbeat, there's a prayer.
We wait, we yearn, we dare believe,
In miracles we can't conceive.

For though the fear sits by our side,
Hope refuses to subside.
It lingers here, within this space,
A quiet glow, a tender grace.

We hold on tight to what we know,
That love is stronger than the woe.
And though the waiting room feels long,
Hope hums beneath, steady and strong.

So, in this place of silent fears,
Where faith is built on hidden tears,
The waiting room becomes a light,
A quiet hope through endless night.

Hands That Save, Hearts That Ache

To the hands that save in darkest hours,
In moments frail, where courage towers—
Thank you, medics, for all you give,
For helping broken souls to live.

Your hands move fast, your minds are clear,
When chaos strikes and danger's near.
You stitch the wounds, you ease the pain,
You hold the line where life remains.

But though your hands are strong and sure,
We know the weight that you endure.
For every life you cannot save,
Leaves echoes deep, a silent wave.

Your hearts, they ache with every call,
With every loss, with every fall.
Yet still you rise, again, again,
To heal the hurt, to soothe the pain.

You carry more than anyone knows,
The silent burden as it grows.
Yet through it all, you stand so brave,
With hands that heal and hearts that save.

So, here's to you, the ones who care,
The medics answering every prayer.
For every life you've pulled from fear,
We thank you now, we hold you dear.

Your hands may save, your hearts may ache,
But through it all, you never break.
And though the world may never see,
You are the hope in misery.

So, thank you for the lives you mend,
For being more than just a friend.
For hands that save and hearts that ache
You are the light when lives forsake.

The Roar of Sirens, the Quiet of Night

In the quiet of night, when the world's asleep,
And the streets lie still, and shadows creep,
A sudden roar breaks through the air
The sirens call, the brave prepare.

Through empty roads and darkened skies,
First responders rise and fly.
With flashing lights and hearts of steel,
They answer every urgent appeal.

The roar of sirens cuts the dark,
A beacon bright, a burning spark.
In every scream, in every cry,
They rush ahead, they don't ask why.

Into the fire, through shattered glass,
Through storms where others dare not pass,
They stand their ground, they fight the flame,
No moment too great, no life the same.

But in the quiet after dawn,
When the sirens fade and chaos's gone,
They carry more than just their gear
The weight of all they've seen, the fear.

For though the night returns to peace,
Their hearts, they race, they never cease.
They hold the scars of lives they've touched,
Of battles fought, of hands they've clutched.

Yet still they stand, with heads held high,
First to answer, first to try.
For every night, when sirens roar,
They'll run again, to face the war.

So, here's to them, the ones who fight
In the roar of sirens, the quiet of night.
First responders, strong and true
We rest in peace because of you.

The Bravery Behind the Badge

It's more than metal, more than shine,
This badge they wear, this sacred sign.
For every time they walk the line,
There's bravery we can't define.

Behind the badge, a heart beats strong,
A warrior's will to right the wrong.
Through city streets or country lanes,
They face the fear, endure the strain.

The badge may gleam beneath the sun,
But bravery's the battle won.
It's in the steps they take each day,
To stand where danger makes its play.

It's in the choice to serve, protect,
To hold the world when it's unchecked.
Behind the badge, a life is sworn,
To face the storm, to brave the thorn.

Each call they answer, sight unseen,
A hero's work, though rarely seen.
Behind the badge, the courage grows,
In every place the darkness goes.

But still, they stand, without retreat,
With every step, with steady feet.
For though the world may shake and spin,
Their bravery lies deep within.

It's in the silence after the call,
When duty's weight begins to fall.
The badge they wear, it cannot show
The battles fought, the pain they know.

Yet still they rise, day after day,
Behind the badge, they find their way.
For bravery is more than fight
It's standing tall through endless night.

So, honor those behind the shield,
Whose hearts and hands will never yield.
The bravery behind the badge,
Is more than steel it's courage unmatched.

A Daughter's Pride in Her Father's Sacrifice

I see it in his eyes, the weight he bears,
The quiet strength, the silent prayers.
My father, standing tall and true,
With a heart that beats red, white, and blue.

He never speaks of battles fought,
Of all the lessons pain has taught.
But I can see it in his face
The scars that time cannot erase.

He gave so much, he left behind
A part of him, both heart and mind.
For country, for honor, for something greater,
He stood as protector, defender, creator.

And though he came home, battle-worn,
A piece of him stayed in the storm.
But through it all, through fire and strife,
I see the sacrifice of his life.

Yet when I look at him, I don't see loss
I see a man who bore the cross.
Who fought so others could be free,
Who gave the world a better me.

I'm proud of him in every way,
For the quiet price he chose to pay.
He stood when others couldn't stand,
With courage carved from hardened hands.

And though the world may never know
The depths of what he let go,
In my heart, he'll always be
The hero he was meant to be.

For in his sacrifice, I find
A strength that ties both heart and mind.
A father's love, a daughter's pride,
His sacrifice forever by my side.

So here I stand, with head held high,
Grateful for the reason why.
For every step he took, I see
His sacrifice lives on in me.

When Everyone Runs from Fire,
My Dad Runs Straight In

When the flames rise high and the heat grows wild,
When the world pulls back in fear, beguiled
There's one who stands, with steady feet,
Who runs toward the burning heat.

My dad, so brave, with helmet tight,
Runs headfirst into the night.
While others flee, they cry, they shout,
He's there to fight, to pull them out.

The crackling fire, the smoky air,
He faces all without a care.
His heart is full of something more,
A strength that opens every door.

I watch him now, with eyes so wide,
And feel a swell of endless pride.
For when the world turns cold with dread,
My dad steps forward, calm instead.

The flames, they dance, they try to win,
But my dad won't let them in.
He battles through the fiercest blaze,
With courage bright, like summer's rays.

And someday soon, when I am grown,
I'll follow him where fires are sown.
I'll wear the helmet, strong and true,
And fight like Dad in skies of blue.

When everyone runs from fire's fierce grin,
I'll run just like my dad straight in.
For in his steps, I'll learn to be
The hero that he taught to me.

So here I stand, his shadow tall,
Dreaming of the day I'll heed the call.
To fight the flames, to rise above
Just like my dad, with heart and love.

The Unspoken Words in a Soldier's Eyes

There are stories deep in a soldier's eyes,
Where silence holds what words disguise.
A thousand tales, both dark and bright,
Of battles fought in day and night.

No voice can shape the things they've seen,
The places where they've walked between
The line of life, the edge of loss
The quiet pain, the heavy cost.

In their gaze, a truth remains,
Of brothers lost and unseen chains.
For in each glance, a memory hides
Of lands they left, of hearts that cried.

The words they don't speak linger long,
In silent strength, in standing strong.
For every step, for every mile,
Is burdened with a knowing smile.

They cannot say what's in their heart,
For where to begin, where to start?
The eyes, they tell what lips can't form,
The quiet hurt, the unseen storm.

And though they smile, and though they stand,
With honor firm, with steady hand,
There's something there, just out of sight,
A depth that lingers in the night.

A soldier's eyes hold all they've known,
The battles fought, the seeds they've sown.
They carry love, they carry pain,
The unspoken words that still remain.

So, look beyond the simple glance,
And see the weight, the circumstance.
For in those eyes, you'll realize—
The soul of war is where it lies.

The Battle That Never Leaves the Mind

The war is over, the fight is done,
But the battle's never truly won.
For though the guns have ceased to fire,
The mind still walks through fields of wire.

In silent hours, in dreams so deep,
The memories stir, they never sleep.
The echoes of a distant land
Still grip the heart, still take command.

Each step they take in peaceful streets,
They hear the drum of marching feet.
Though safe at home, though loved ones near,
The past returns, sharp and clear.

The battle that never leaves the mind
Is not the kind that fate can bind.
It lingers long, it takes its toll,
It etches scars upon the soul.

The flashes come, the nights grow cold,
The fear they thought they'd long controlled.
In quiet rooms, in gentle rain,
The ghosts of war still bring their pain.

For every moment on the field
Becomes a wound that won't be healed.
And though they smile, and though they try,
The battle hides behind their eyes.

The fight is not with sword or gun,
But with the mind that won't outrun
The shadows of what once had been,
The sights and sounds that pull them in.

Yet still they rise, still they press on,
Even when the light feels gone.
For in their hearts, a strength remains
To bear the weight of unseen chains.

The battle that never leaves the mind
Is a war of a different kind.
But through it all, they stand so strong
Fighting for peace, where they belong.

Strength Forged in Fire and Fear

In the heart of the flame, where the world turns
wild,
Where fear grips tight and danger's riled,
There rises a strength, unseen, untold,
A spirit forged in heat and cold.

Through fire's blaze and fear's dark grip,
Where hands may tremble, minds may slip,
A warrior stands, though the flames burn high,
Their strength born from the battle cry.

For in the fear, they find their steel,
In every blaze, in every reel.
The sweat, the pain, the scars they bear,
Forge something strong beyond compare.

They walk through fire, face the storm,
Where most would flee, they take their form.
In every test, in every tear,
Their strength is born from fire and fear.

It's not in running, not in flight,
But standing tall in darkest night.
For in those moments, raw and true,
They find the strength to see it through.

And when the flames have died away,
And fear no longer holds its sway,
The strength remains, unshaken still,
Forged by fire, and fear, and will.

So, here's to those who face the fight,
Whose strength is born from darkest night.
For in the flames and fear they tread,
They rise with courage, burning red.

Strength forged in fire, in fear so deep,
A warrior's soul, forever to keep.

The Flag Folded, a Nation Mourns

The bugle plays its solemn sound,
As loved ones gather all around.
A Marine lies in honored rest,
Their bravery worn upon their chest.

The flag is folded, sharp and tight,
Red, white, and blue beneath the light.
With every fold, a story told
Of battles fought, of hearts so bold.

A nation mourns in quiet grace,
For the Marine who took their place.
They stood where others dared not go,
In lands where only courage grows.

Through storms of fire, through endless night,
They fought with everything in sight.
And now they rest, their duty done,
A hero lost, a battle won.

The flag is handed, slow and sure,
A symbol of the fight they bore.
And as it passes into hands,
A nation weeps, yet still it stands.

For every fold, a tear is shed,
For those who served, for those now dead.
Yet in the mourning, there's a pride
A Marine whose honor will not die.

Though they have fallen, still they rise,
In memories, in tear-filled eyes.
The flag that waves, though folded here,
Will fly for them, year after year.

So, as we mourn, we stand and know
The courage they had, the seeds they sow.
The flag is folded, a life laid down,
But in their place, we hold the crown.

For every Marine who gave their all,
We stand together, proud and tall.
The flag folded, a nation mourns,
But their spirit in our hearts is born.

The Weight of the World on a Single Shoulder

To be the president, the leader bold,
Is more than power, more than gold.
It's waking up to endless strife,
A constant battle, a constant life.

The weight of the world on a single shoulder,
A heart must be strong, a mind much older.
For every step, a choice is made,
Where history's path is firmly laid.

The voices call from every side,
A nation's hopes, too vast to hide.
Decisions made in silent rooms,
Where light feels dim and shadows loom.

It's shaking hands, it's speaking clear,
It's facing every doubt and fear.
It's standing tall when storms arise,
While seeing truth in countless eyes.

To be the president means to bear
The dreams of millions everywhere.
To listen close, to hold what's true,
Yet carry scars no one can view.

For in the quiet, in the night,
When stars grow dim and fade from sight,
The weight grows heavy, hard to bear
Yet still, they rise and face the air.

It's more than laws or speeches grand,
It's feeling every outstretched hand.
The weight of the world on a single soul,
To bind a nation, to make it whole.

To lead with wisdom, heart, and grace,
While running a never-ending race.
For every burden, every tear,
Falls on the one who stands right here.

Yet still, they rise, they take their stand,
To guide the fate of this great land.
The weight of the world, so vast, so deep,
Yet on their shoulders, it will keep.

For to be the president, to lead the way,
Is to carry the night and forge the day.

The First Responders, Running into the Unknown

When the sirens wail and the streets fall still,
When fear takes hold and the air turns chill,
There are those who rise without delay
The first responders, on their way.

Into the unknown, where danger lies,
Where flames reach up to the darkened skies,
Where chaos reigns and hearts feel fear,
They press ahead, they draw near.

They run toward what others flee,
Through smoke, through fire, through misery.
With steady hands and steadfast eyes,
They face the world as it divides.

For every step, a risk they take,
For every life, a choice they make.
They rush into the darkest night,
To be the spark, to be the light.

They do not know what waits ahead,
If they'll return, or face what's dead.
Yet still they go, without a pause
To serve, protect, it's in their cause.

The unknown calls, the shadows rise,
But courage lives where duty ties.
The first responders, bold and true,
Run into the dark for me, for you.

So, here's to them, the brave, the strong,
Who run to where they don't belong.
For in their hearts, a fire grows
To save, to heal, no matter the unknown.

There Are No Words That Will Ever Do

There are no words that will ever do,
No thank you, gift, or ribbon true.
No medal shining, bright or bold,
Can match the sacrifice they hold.

For those who fight for freedom's name,
Who bear the cost, who take the blame,
Who stand where others turn away,
And hold the line, come night or day.

The red, the white, the blue, they bear,
In every step, in every prayer.
They give their lives, they give their all,
So, we may rise, so we may stand tall.

What can we say? What can we give
To those who fight, who die, who live
With scars and stories left untold,
Of courage fierce, of hearts so bold?

No words can ever fill the space,
Of those who fight with honor, grace.
No gesture made, no gift of gold
Can match the lives that they behold.

They stand for freedom, night and day,
In lands afar, so far away.
They guard the flag, they keep us free,
They fight for you; they fight for me.

And so, we try, with all our might,
To honor them, to speak of their fight.
But words will falter, gifts will fade
For their true worth can't be repaid.

There are no words that will ever do,
No thank you strong, no ribbon new.
But still, we stand, with hearts sincere,
To say to them, "We hold you dear."

For in the red, the white, the blue,
Their strength, their love, forever true.
And though no words can be enough,
We thank them with our endless love.

The Child Who Learns Bravery from Their Hero Parent

In quiet moments, side by side,
A hero's heart is magnified.
A child watches, eyes so wide,
As courage blooms, as fears subside.

Their parent stands, so brave and true,
With every step, they learn anew.
The way to face the world so strong,
To right the wrong, to carry on.

In every word, in every deed,
A hero plants the deepest seed
Of strength and love, of standing tall,
Of knowing how to rise and fall.

The child learns in ways unspoken,
Through silent acts, through hearts unbroken.
For bravery's not just in the fight,
But in the love that shines so bright.

They watch, they learn, they slowly grow,
And soon, the seeds of courage show.
For in their parent's every move,
A legacy begins to prove.

And when the time comes, they will stand,
With bravery held in their hand.
A new generation, bold and free,
Carrying forward the legacy.

For bravery's passed from heart to heart,
From parent's strength, a child's start.
A cycle endless, ever strong,
That carries love and courage on.

So here they stand, the child grown,
With lessons learned, with seeds now sown.
Bravery lives, through every fight
A hero's gift, passed on in light.

The Spouse Who Wears Courage Like a Second Skin

They stand in shadows, quiet, strong,
The spouse who waits while days grow long.
With every call, with every task,
They wear their courage like a mask.

But deeper still, beneath the smile,
Is bravery that runs the mile.
For when their love must go away,
It's courage that begins to stay.

They hold the fort, they bear the weight,
They fight the fear, defy the fate.
Through sleepless nights and silent prayers,
Their strength remains, though no one stares.

Courage wraps them, head to toe,
A second skin they've come to know.
It shields the heart when tears arise,
It holds them firm when hope defies.

They never asked for battles fierce,
For days apart, for hearts to pierce.
But still they stand, with love so true,
A quiet hero in all they do.

For every day they wait alone,
Their strength becomes a cornerstone.
No uniform, no badge, no gear
But courage carried year to year.

So, here's to them, the ones who stay,
Who wear their courage day by day.
The spouses strong, through thick and thin,
Who wear their love like second skin.

A Soldier's Love Letter, Written in the Sand

A soldier kneels with steady hand,
To trace their love upon the sand.
No pen, no paper, just the shore
A message sent from heart's deep core.

Each stroke a promise, soft and true,
A love that stretches skyward, too.
With every line, with every word,
The silence of the soul is heard.

Footprints trail where once they stood,
A soldier walking where they could
Across the land, through dust and time,
Their heartbeats steady, battle's rhyme.

But here, in moments still and clear,
They carve their love, they hold it near.
A sniper's heart, in sand is drawn,
The marks of war, the edge of dawn.

For though they fight, for though they stand,
Their love remains within the sand.
A soldier's heart, though far away,
Still writes the words they long to say.

In quiet winds, their message drifts,
A love that never bends or shifts.
The footprints fade, the tide rolls near,
But love, once written, won't disappear.

A soldier's love letter, left behind,
In grains of sand, for hearts to find.
Though miles may stretch, and time may tear,
Their love remains, written there.

Quiet Hero, Never Asking for Praise

A quiet hero walks among us all,
No trumpet's sound, no grand hall.
No shining light, no loud acclaim,
Yet bravery burns without a name.

They stand where others fear to tread,
With steady heart and quiet tread.
They lift the weight when no one sees,
And carry burdens with unseen ease.

No need for cheers, no call for fame,
No need for medals or a claim.
For in their heart, they know their way
To serve, to give, without delay.

When troubles rise or shadows fall,
They answer softly, standing tall.
Not seeking glory, gold, or gain,
Just helping others through their pain.

They give their all, and then some more,
A strength that echoes to the core.
But never once do they demand
A lifted voice, a clapping hand.

A quiet hero, strong and true,
In every act, in all they do.
They ask for nothing, yet they give
A silent love in how they live.

So, here's to them, in quiet grace,
The ones who never seek a place
Among the stars, or in the light,
Yet shine in darkness, pure and bright.

A quiet hero, brave and kind,
Their strength forever intertwined
With acts of love, both big and small
A hero's heart, unseen by all.

Sacrifice Written in Every Line of a Face

In every wrinkle, every scar,
A story lives of battles far.
The lines upon a weathered face,
Are etched with sacrifice and grace.

No words are needed to explain,
The weight of love, the cost of pain.
For in those lines, both deep and true,
Lies every sacrifice they knew.

The sleepless nights, the heavy load,
The quiet paths they've always strode.
The moments lost, the tears held back,
The silent strength when courage lacked.

The lines tell tales of years gone by,
Of times they fought, of times they cried.
Of love for country, love for kin,
Of battles waged without, within.

Each furrow marks a choice they made,
Each crease, a price that has been paid.
For freedom's cost is often told
In faces growing worn and old.

But in those lines, there's honor too,
For every battle they've been through.
A life of service, carved in skin,
A testament to where they've been.

So look upon that face with pride,
For sacrifice cannot be denied.
It's written there for all to see,
The quiet cost of bravery.

In every line, in every crease,
A part of them that's found release.
Sacrifice, worn deep and plain,
A face that speaks of love and pain.

The Weight of the Badge Rests Heavy on My Chest

The badge I wear is more than steel,
It's a symbol of the oath I feel.
A silent promise, strong and true,
To serve, protect, and see it through.

It shines beneath the morning sun,
But its weight is felt when day is done.
For every call, for every task,
It holds the questions I never ask.

The weight of the badge rests heavy on my chest,
A burden taken with every step.
Not for the glory, not for the fame,
But for the lives I guard in honor's name.

In every shift, in every night,
I feel its pull, both wrong and right.
It reminds me why I made this choice—
To be a shield, to be a voice.

But with each rescue, each moment passed,
I carry the faces that may not last.
The ones I couldn't help in time,
The echoes of a silent crime.

Yet still I stand, through storm and strife,
For in this badge, there's more than life.
It holds the hope of those in fear,
The weight of love, so bright and clear.

The weight of the badge, though heavy to bear,
Is the price I pay because I care.
And though it pulls, and though it strains,
I'll wear it proudly through the pain.

For in its weight, I find my way,
To serve with honor, day by day.
The badge rests heavy, yes, it's true—
But it's a weight I'll carry through.

My Boots Hit the Ground Before the Sun Rises

My boots hit the ground before the dawn,
Before the birds have sung their song.
The world still sleeps, the sky still dark,
But I'm already moving, making my mark.

Before the sun can light the way,
I'm out there, starting the day.
Through quiet streets and shadows deep,
I walk the path where others sleep.

The weight of duty in each step,
A silent vow that I have kept.
To stand where needed, come what may,
Before the first light breaks the gray.

The morning chill is all I feel,
The echoes of a world so real.
But even when the nights are long,
I know this is where I belong.

For every sunrise that I greet,
There's purpose in my steady feet.
A job to do, a task to face,
To bring a little hope, a little grace.

So long before the world's awake,
My boots hit the ground for others' sake.
I walk the path, I play my part,
With quiet strength and open heart.

The sun will rise, the day will break,
But I'll be ready, for their sake.
My boots hit the ground without a sound,
Before the light, on sacred ground.

Every Call I Answer Is a Promise Kept

Every call that echoes through the night,
Is more than duty, more than might.
It's a promise whispered long ago,
To stand for those who'll never know.

The sirens blare, the voices rise,
But in my heart, the reason lies.
A vow I made when I took this stand,
To lend my strength, to offer my hand.

For every call I answer, swift and true,
Is a promise kept, a duty due.
To be the shield in moments grim,
To fight for them when hope runs thin.

It's not for praise, it's not for fame,
But for the lives I strive to claim.
In every cry, in every plea,
I hear the vow that carries me.

To save, to serve, to guide the way,
In darkest night, or brightest day.
Each call a chance to stand once more,
To be the hope on every shore.

So, when the world begins to sleep,
I rise to keep the promises deep.
For every call, a life may wait,
And I will answer, without debate.

Each time I hear that urgent sound,

I know my purpose, I'm duty-bound.
For every call I answer is a promise kept,
A vow I honor, as others slept.

I Fight for Freedom, but Also for My Family's Future

I stand on distant, foreign ground,
Where freedom's cost is tightly bound.
I fight for liberty, pure and true,
But in my heart, I fight for you.

For every battle that I face,
I see my family's future trace.
The dreams we hold, the life we planned,
Are why I fight in this far-off land.

It's more than flags or banners raised,
More than glory, more than praise.
It's the hope that one day I'll return,
To a world where peace can truly burn.

I fight for freedom, yes, it's clear,
But there's another reason I am here.
For in my mind, I see their eyes
My family waiting under peaceful skies.

I fight for their tomorrow bright,
For mornings safe, for restful night.
For a world where they can walk with pride,
Without the fear that I've defied.

Every step I take, every battle fought,
Is for the future I have sought.
Not just for me, not just for now,
But for them, my love, my solemn vow.

So, as I stand with courage tall,
I know my reason, I know my call.
I fight for freedom, strong and true,
But also for the future I'll build with you.

Behind Every Mission,
There's a Piece of My Heart Left Behind

Behind every mission, a part of me stays,
In the dust of the desert, in the thick of the haze.
I leave my heart in every land,
With every step, with every stand.

The battle calls, I answer swift,
But with each call, I feel the shift.
A piece of my soul, a part of my mind,
Is left behind, hard to find.

In the faces of those I could not save,
In the moments that made me strong, yet brave
I leave a mark, unseen, untold,
In lands of fire, in nights so cold.

Behind every mission, I feel the cost,
The weight of moments loved ones lost.
Yet still I go, with purpose clear,
Knowing my heart will disappear.

Each mission takes a little more,
A part of me left on the floor.
But still I fight, for something true,
For the ones I love, for all of you.

And though the missions may seem to end,
I'll never quite be whole again.
For behind every mission, in every land,
There's a piece of me that stays, unmanned.

But I carry on, with head held high,
Though parts of me still linger by.
For the heart I leave, I know is mine
A soldier's love left behind.

The Flag on My Sleeve Carries All the Stories of Those Who Fell Before Me

The flag on my sleeve is more than thread,
It holds the stories of the dead.
Of those who stood where now I stand,
Who gave their lives for this great land.

Each star, each stripe, a tale untold,
Of battles fought, of hearts so bold.
The flag I wear upon my sleeve
Is heavy with the souls who grieve.

It carries whispers in the breeze,
Of soldiers lost across the seas.
Of heroes' brave, whose names I know
Are etched in fields where poppies grow.

When I wear this flag, I bear their fight,
Their silent march, their endless night.
The ones who fell before I came,
Their sacrifice, my steady flame.

For every step, I hear their call,
The weight of freedom paid by all.
And though I walk with steady stride,
Their legacy walks by my side.

The flag upon my arm may wave,
But it's a symbol of the brave.
Of those who fell so I could rise,
And see the world with open eyes.

So, as I wear this flag with pride,
I carry those who never died.
In every stitch, their stories lie
Of heroes' hearts, of last goodbyes.

The flag on my sleeve is not just mine,
It's woven through with sacrifice and time.
It holds the stories, pure and true,
Of all who fell for red, white, and blue.

I Run Toward the Flames, Because Someone Has To

I run toward the flames, because someone must,
Into the smoke, the heat, the dust.
Where others flee, I find my place,
To stand against the fire's embrace.

The world behind me shouts and screams,
But I push forward through burning dreams.
The flames may rise, the walls may fall,
Yet still I answer every call.

It's not for glory, not for fame,
But for the lives that call my name.
For those who wait, for those who fear,
I run toward the danger near.

The heat is fierce, the air is thin,
But I refuse to let it win.
For in my heart, I know it's true
I run toward the flames for you.

The courage comes, though fear is near,
I face the fire; I fight the fear.
Because someone has to take the stand,
To pull you from the fire's hand.

I run toward the flames, I won't turn back,
Through blazing heat, through skies of black.
For in the fire, I find my way
To save a life, to see the day.

So, when you see the flames rise high,
Know there's someone who will try.
I run toward the flames, it's what I do
Because someone has to, and I choose to.

I May Stand Alone in the Night,
but I Am Never Truly Alone

I may stand alone in the quiet night,
Where darkness falls and dims the light.
But in my heart, I know they're near
My family's love, so strong, so dear.

God's presence fills the air around,
In every breath, His grace is found.
Jesus walks beside me, calm and true,
Guiding me in all I do.

Though shadows creep and fears arise,
I feel His strength, I see His eyes.
With angels guarding every side,
Their wings spread wide, they will not hide.

At four corners, they stand so bright,
A shield of love through every fight.
And the Holy Spirit, soft and clear,
Whispers truth that I hold dear.

God's hand upon my soul, so wide,
With Jesus walking by my side.
The Holy Spirit as my guide,
And angels watching, arms open wide.

So, though I may stand in the night alone,
I am never truly on my own.
For in my heart, my family stays,
And God lights up my darkest days.

Jesus holds me with gentle grace,
And angels guard my every space.
The Holy Spirit leads me through,
In all I face, in all I do.

I may stand alone, but never in fear,
For God and Jesus are always near.
With angels and the Spirit bright,
I walk in love, I walk in light.

Each Goodbye is Harder than the Last

Each goodbye is harder than the last,
As moments slip into the past.
I hold you close, then let you go,
With every tear, the love will grow.

The words come soft, the time feels near,
And in your eyes, I see the fear.
Yet still, you stand with head held high,
But in my heart, I want to cry.

The bags are packed, the door is wide,
I feel the pull, the ache inside.
For every time we say goodbye,
A little piece of us must die.

The first goodbye was full of hope,
But now I barely seem to cope.
For with each tour, with each return,
The flame of worry seems to burn.

But duty calls, and so you go,
Into the unknown, far below.
And though I stay, I feel the strain,
The weight of love, the quiet pain.

I say goodbye, but not for long,
In every tear, you still belong.
Each time you leave, the heartache's vast
Each goodbye is harder than the last.

Yet still I wait, and still I pray,
For you to come home safe one day.
Until that time, I hold on fast
Knowing each goodbye won't be the last.

When I Serve, My Family Serves Too

When I put on this uniform and stand so tall,
It's not just me who answers the call.
For every step I take, so true,
I know my family is serving too.

They may not wear the badge or fight,
But they bear the weight of every night.
The sleepless hours, the worry and strain,
Their hearts feel every ounce of pain.

When I serve, they stand with me,
In quiet strength and loyalty.
They hold the home while I'm away,
And carry the burden every day.

In every letter, in every prayer,
Their love is with me everywhere.
Their sacrifice, though rarely seen,
Is woven in every in-between.

For when I serve, it's not just me
It's my family's courage, silently.
They give their all, they hold the line,
Their strength and love, forever mine.

So, though I wear the uniform proud,
It's my family's honor, strong and loud.
When I serve, they serve with grace
Together, we hold our sacred place.

**It's Not the Uniform That Defines Me,
but the Purpose It Holds**

It's not the uniform that defines my soul,
Not the badges bright, nor the buttons bold.
It's not the cloth that makes me stand,
But the purpose placed in my steady hand.

For beyond the threads and stripes I wear,
Lies something deeper, something rare.
A duty, a calling, a promise made,
A life I've chosen, a path I've paved.

The uniform's a symbol, strong and true,
But it's the heart that pulls me through.
It's not the fabric stitched so fine,
But the reason, the cause, the guiding line.

I serve because I believe in more,
In protecting lives, in stopping war.
In lifting those who've fallen low,
In being the light when darkness grows.

The uniform may catch the eye,
But it's the mission that makes me try.
It's not the clothing, nor the gear
It's the purpose driving away my fear.

For when I serve, I do it all
For something greater, for duty's call.
It's not the uniform that defines me whole,
But the purpose that burns within my soul.

The Radio Crackles, and I Know It's Time to Move

The radio crackles, a sudden sound,
Breaking through the quiet ground.
In that moment, without a doubt,
I know it's time to bug out.

The silence shatters, tension grows,
Where the next step leads, no one knows.
In a heartbeat, we pack and run,
Underneath the rising sun.

We move fast, no time to waste,
Every second, every breath, a frantic pace.
For in the distance, danger looms,
And in its shadow, the threat consumes.

The world turns sharp, the lines are drawn,
In every step, we carry on.
The gear is heavy, the ground is rough,
But we are trained, and we are tough.

The radio calls, the signal's clear
It's time to go, the threat is near.
With every crackle, every word,
The urgency inside is stirred.

We leave behind what's not essential,
Our minds are sharp, our focus mental.
For when the radio's voice commands,
We understand the shifting sands.

We move with purpose, with silent speed,
Responding to the nation's need.
For in this life, we know too well
That peace can break, and chaos swell.

The radio crackles, and we know our role,
To stay on guard, to keep control.
At any moment, we're ready to prove
When the call comes, it's time to move.

I Didn't Choose the Easy Path,
but I Wouldn't Trade It for Anything

I didn't choose the easy way,
Where comfort reigns and troubles sway.
I chose a path that's rough and steep,
Where sleepless nights and promises keep.

I didn't pick the road of rest,
But one that puts me to the test.
Each step I take is filled with strain,
But I'd do it all and do it again.

The easy path was never mine,
For in my heart, I drew the line
To stand for something, bold and true,
To give my all in all I do.

I didn't choose the quiet days,
But ones where courage leads the way.
Through storms, through fire, I have walked,
But every trial has left me awed.

I wouldn't trade this life, this call,
For any comfort, none at all.
The easy path may seem so sweet,
But this is where my heart's complete.

For in the struggle, in the fight,
I've found my purpose, found my light.
The harder road has made me strong,
And here, I know I truly belong.

I didn't choose the easy path,
But I've found joy in every wrath.
For what I've gained, for what I've seen,
I wouldn't trade it for a dream.

Each Mission Takes a Part of Me, but It Gives Something Back Too

Each mission takes a part of me,
A piece that's lost across the sea.
A fragment of my heart and soul,
Left behind to make me whole.

The battles fought, the sleepless nights,
The endless march through distant fights.
They take their toll, they weigh me down,
But still, I rise, without a frown.

For every step I give away,
There's something more I gain each day.
A lesson learned, a bond made tight,
A deeper strength to guide my fight.

Though I lose myself in what I give,
The purpose grows in how I live.
Each mission strips away the old,
And leaves me braver, strong, and bold.

It takes a part, yet gives me more
A sense of what I'm fighting for.
A clearer view of who I am,
A soldier bound to a greater plan.

The price is high, I feel the strain,
But through the loss, I still sustain.
For every piece that's given free,
It's replaced by something deep in me.

Each mission takes a part, it's true,
But it gives something back to you.
The sacrifice, the road I tread,
Has filled my soul with hope instead.

And though the cost is never light,
I wouldn't change this sacred fight.
For in the taking, I receive
A greater purpose, I believe.

I Fight Not for Glory,
but for Peace That Few Will Ever See

I don't fight for the cheers or fame,
Nor for the medals or a name.
I don't seek glory, bright and loud,
To stand apart or please the crowd.

I fight for something quiet, small,
A peace that rises after all.
A peace so few will ever know,
That whispers softly as I go.

For in the chaos, in the strife,
I carry hope, I guard the life
Of futures waiting to unfold,
In moments calm, in hands to hold.

It's not the battle or the roar,
But the peace that follows every war.
The silence after skies have cleared,
The dreams rebuilt; the lives endeared.

I fight for homes untouched by fear,
For children laughing, futures clear.
For mornings where the sun can rise,
Without the smoke in endless skies.

I fight not for the claim of fame,
But for a world that stays the same
Where love can grow, where hearts are free,
A peace that few will ever see.

Though they may never know my name,
Nor understand the path I claim,
I fight for peace, for all that's true,
For futures bright, for skies of blue.

So as I stand and face the fight,
I know my reason, know my light.
Not for the glory or acclaim,
But for the peace that ends the flame.

There's Honor in Standing Where Others Cannot

There's honor in standing where others can't go,
In the face of the fear, in the depths of the unknown.
Where the ground shakes and the winds roar high,
I plant my feet, I won't pass by.

When the weight is too heavy, the cost too great,
I find my strength, I hold my fate.
For there's a calling, silent but clear,
To stand in the place where danger is near.

Not everyone can walk this road,
Where the burdens are heavy, the risks untold.
But here I am, through the thick and thin,
Finding the courage that lies within.

It's not for glory or for praise,
But for the lives I save in countless ways.
For every moment I stand my ground,
I know there's honor to be found.

In the spaces others cannot tread,
I stand with hope, where fear is fed.
There's something deeper in the fight,
An honor born from doing right.

So here I stand, strong and tall,
In places where the brave may fall.
For there's honor in standing where others cannot,
In facing the fire, no matter the cost.

A Simple Box Renews My Faith

A simple box, wrapped with care,
Arrives with hope through desert air.
You may not think it matters much,
But to me, it's a heart-warmed touch.

Oh, the box sent from home, so true,
With cookies, cards, and comfort too.
Inside, the treasures that make me smile
A piece of home across the miles.

Toiletries like soap and shampoo,
Body wash, toothpaste, floss for a crew.
Toothbrush, deodorant, lip balm, hand sanitizer
Each small item feels like a prized reminder.

Comfort comes in socks and flips,
Sunblock for the burning trips.
Hand warmers when the nights grow cold,
And underwear, a gift of gold.

Snacks tucked in, a joy to see
Chips, salsa, nuts, beef jerky.
Cookies, candy that doesn't melt,
Trail mix too, and comfort felt.

Home touches like coffee, familiar and warm,
A baseball game program, photos of charm.
A card with words that feel so real,
In the desert, it's Christmas, and I finally feel

For a moment, I'm back where I belong,
In a place where nothing feels too wrong.
Writing material for thoughts to share
Envelopes, stamps, and paper to spare.

Pens and pencils for lines I'll send,
Back to the ones who are more than friends.
A mini tree, or Halloween treat,
Or Easter eggs, sweet and discreet.

A simple box renews my faith,
A reminder of home, love, and grace.
In this desert, where time drags on,
It's a moment of peace, where my heart is drawn.

So, thank you for the thought, the care,
For sending love in a box I wear.
It may seem small, but it's more than enough
A simple box filled with love and trust.

I Walk Into the Unknown with Only Hope in My Heart

I walk into the unknown, no map to guide,
With shadows stretching far and wide.
The path ahead, I cannot see,
But still I go, with hope in me.

No promises of what's to come,
No certainty beneath the sun.
Yet step by step, I push ahead,
With hope alive where fear once bled.

For in my heart, a quiet flame,
A trust in what I cannot name.
It keeps me strong, it pulls me through,
When all around seems cold and blue.

I walk into the dark, the storm,
With only hope to keep me warm.
For though the road is rough and steep,
It's hope that holds me as I leap.

I do not know what lies ahead,
But hope is where my soul is led.
I carry it in every stride,
With faith and love deep inside.

So, into the unknown I will go,
With hope the only guide I know.
It lights the way, though faint and small
It's hope that lifts me through it all.

The Sound of the Siren Is a Call I'll Always Answer

The sound of the siren cuts through the air,
A cry for help, a call to care.
It echoes loud, it pulls me near,
To face the danger, to fight the fear.

I hear its wail, and my heart stands tall,
For the siren's song is a duty call.
In every beat, in every tone,
I know it's time, I'm not alone.

No matter the hour, no matter the cost,
I'll answer the call, no moment lost.
Through smoke and fire, through storm and rain,
I'll rise again, despite the strain.

The siren calls where courage leads,
And I will run where bravery pleads.
For every life, for every soul,
The sound of the siren makes me whole.

It's more than noise, it's more than fear,
It's the reason why I'm always here.
To serve, to save, to stand my ground,
When the siren calls, I'm honor bound.

So let it wail, let it cry,
I'll never question, I'll never deny.
The sound of the siren is my cue
A call I'll always answer, strong and true.

This Job Changes You,
but You Hope It Changes You for the Better

This job, it shapes you, day by day,
In ways you never thought it may.
The things you see, the weight you bear,
Leave marks that linger everywhere.

You walk through fear, you stand through pain,
In every loss, in every gain.
Each call you answer, every fight,
It changes something deep inside.

It hardens parts, it makes you tough,
Sometimes the road feels more than rough.
But in the end, you hope and pray,
It shapes you in a better way.

For every life that you've helped save,
For every moment you've stood brave,
You find a piece of something true
The strength you didn't know was you.

The days grow long, the nights seem fast,
But through it all, you hold steadfast.
You hope that through the trials you face,
You've learned to fill the world with grace.

This job, it changes who you are,
It leaves behind a lasting scar.
But through the cracks, you hope to find
A better heart, a stronger mind.

So as the days turn into years,
And you confront your deepest fears,
You hold on to the quiet dream,
That you've become who you're meant to be.

I Live for the Moments When I Can Save a Life

I live for the moments when I can save a life,
Amidst all the chaos, the struggle, the strife.
For all the death and sorrow, I see,
I only count the ones I helped to breathe.

The darkness comes, the pain is real,
The weight of loss is hard to feel.
But in the quiet, through the tears,
I hold on to those precious years.

The times I fought, the lives I won,
Those fleeting moments in the sun.
When someone gasped and found the air,
And I was there, to show I care.

For every loss that haunts my mind,
It's the saved ones I seek to find.
I carry their faces, their breath, their smiles,
Through endless nights and endless miles.

In the sorrow, in the fear,
I keep those moments crystal clear.
For every hand I held so tight,
There's one I pulled into the light.

I live for the moments, few and bright,
When hope returns, when hearts ignite.
For in a world of grief and strife,
I live for the chance to save a life.

There's No Manual for the Emotions
That Come with This Work

There's no manual for the things we feel,
For the scars that time can't seem to heal.
The weight we carry, the silent pain,
The thoughts that run like endless rain.

You could talk to someone, open wide,
But most don't hear what's locked inside.
They're busy, caught up in their own race,
Never seeing the burden, you face.

And "I'm fine" becomes a practiced phrase,
A shield we wear on heavy days.
But don't take those words and walk away
There's so much more we're trying to say.

So, take a moment, lend your ear,
Turn off your phone, just be near.
Let the world slow down for a while,
And truly listen, without a mile.

When a veteran speaks, it's not just words,
It's echoes of all the things unheard.
So, stay awhile, even if it's late,
Let them share, let them relate.

Don't rush away, don't cut them short,
Their stories need a full report.
And even if they say they're fine,
Look in their eyes read between the lines.

It may take time for them to trust,
But be present, because you must.
Even if it's midnight's clock,
Just sit with them and let them talk.

There's no manual for what we feel,
But you can help us start to heal.
By showing up and staying still,
You give us space; you give us will.

So, listen close, take time to see
The weight we carry silently.
And know your presence means so much
To those of us who've lost the touch.

I Leave My Fear Behind When I Step Into the Field

I leave my fear behind, far and wide,
When I step into the field with steady stride.
The weight of worry, the fear of fall,
Fades away when duty calls.

For in this space, there's no room for doubt,
Only the mission I'm thinking about.
The chaos, the storm, the risk so near
But I walk forward, leaving fear.

I've learned to trust the strength inside,
The courage that fear cannot divide.
Though danger lurks, though shadows loom,
I face the fight; I embrace the room.

My heart may race, my hands may shake,
But when I'm out there, I don't break.
I let my training guide the way,
And let my purpose lead the day.

For in the field, it's more than me,
It's the lives I guard, it's what must be.
I walk with courage, bold and clear
I leave my fear behind, right here.

So, when I step into the field again,
I know my fear is not my end.
For I've learned to stand, learned to fight,
And trust in the power of the light.

I leave my fear behind, it fades,
As I walk forward through the blades.
With every step, I rise and feel—
The strength that makes my courage real.

Serving Means Sacrifice, but It's One I Make Willingly

Serving means sacrifice, that much is true,
But it's one I make, knowing what I do.
There are moments, of course, when I long for home,
For familiar faces and streets I've known.

But when those moments come, I close my eyes,
And in my heart, I visualize
My mother's smile, my sister's grace,
My children's laughter, my father's face.

My brother's strength, my aunt June's care,
The love that waits for me back there.
In those memories, I find my way,
To stand my ground, come what may.

For every day, I answer the call,
To protect them all, one and all.
Though the road is long, and the cost is steep,
Their safety is the vow I keep.

I fight for them, through night and day,
For their tomorrows, I'll make a way.
And when I'm weary, far from home,
I close my eyes, and I'm not alone.

Serving means sacrifice, that's what I've known,
But I do it willingly, even when I'm gone.
For in my heart, they're always near
And for their future, I have no fear.

So, I stand my ground, with purpose clear,
To protect them all, year after year.
Each time I hear the call to fight,
I do it for their peace, their light.

I Train for the Worst, but I Pray for the Best

I train for the worst, with grit in my bones,
For the darkest of nights, for the coldest of tones.
I prepare for the battle, the chaos, the storm,
For the moments where nothing feels safe or warm.

In every drill, in every step,
I push myself further, no room for regret.
For when the worst comes knocking loud,
I'll be ready to stand, to make my vow.

But while I train for the trials ahead,
I pray for the best instead.
I pray for peace, for calmer days,
For nights that end in softer ways.

I train to face the harshest fight,
But in my heart, I seek the light.
I hope for moments of quiet grace,
For joy to fill each familiar place.

Though I am prepared for what may come,
I dream of a world where fear is done.
Where battles fade, and wars are few
That's the future I pursue.

So, I'll train for the worst, with strength and pride,
But I'll pray for the best to stand by my side.
For in the end, both heart and hand,
I strive for peace in this weary land.

In the Silence After the Call

On rare occasions, we get to call,
A moment's peace to speak with all.
A voice from home, familiar and clear,
Bringing comfort, chasing fear.

I hear their laughter, feel their love,
A precious gift from skies above.
For just a moment, I'm back again,
With family, friends, and all that's been.

We share our stories, short and sweet,
Bridging the miles between our feet.
But soon enough, the call must end,
And I'm left alone, without my friends.

In the silence after the call,
I think of home, I feel it all.
The faces vivid in my mind,
The love I've left so far behind.

The kitchen table, the morning light,
The quiet talks late into the night.
The little things that make it real,
The life I long so much to feel.

Though miles away, in heart I stay,
With those I love, though far away.
In the silence, I hold them near,
Their voices ringing in my ear.

And as the silence softly falls,
I find my strength in those brief calls.
For in my heart, I carry home,
No matter how far I may roam.

The Hardest Part Is Seeing the
Pain I Can't Always Heal

The hardest part of what I do
Isn't the battles I fight through.
It's not the weight of duty's call,
Or standing strong when others fall.

It's seeing the pain I can't always heal,
The wounds too deep, the scars too real.
The silent cries, the hollow eyes,
The hope that fades beneath the skies.

I wish my hands could mend it all,
To lift them up when they feel small.
But some pain runs too deep to touch,
And knowing that, it hurts so much.

I stand and watch, I give my best,
But some hearts break without a rest.
I fight for them, I stand in place,
Yet still I see the tears they face.

I can't heal everything, I know,
And that's the weight I can't let go.
The hardest part, the bitter truth
Is knowing I can't take away the bruise.

But still I stand, I give my care,
For every moment I am there.
Even if I can't heal all,
I'll catch them if they start to fall.

I carry their pain within my chest,
Even when I can't fix the rest.
For though I can't heal every scar,
I'll be the light in the dark, from afar.

**There Are Faces I'll Never Forget,
Both the Saved and the Lost**

There are faces I'll never forget,
Etched in my heart like silhouettes.
Some were saved, their lives regained,
Others lost, forever stained.

I see their eyes in quiet dreams,
Moments frozen, mid-split seams.
The joy of those who found the light,
The sorrow of those who slipped from sight.

The saved, they smile, their breaths renewed,
Their hopes restored; their fears subdued.
I hold their faces close and dear,
A reminder why I'm always here.

But the lost, they linger just as long,
Their presence heavy, deep and strong.
The ones I couldn't pull from fate,
Their memory rests, a heavy weight.

Each one a story, a life untold,
A fleeting moment, brave and bold.
They stay with me, through night and day,
The saved, the lost they never fade away.

There are faces I'll never forget,
Each one a reason, a quiet debt.
Both the victories and the cost,
In every saved and every lost.

It's the Little Things That Keep Me Going
A Laugh, a Smile, a Thank You

It's not the glory or the grand applause,
That fuels my spirit or gives me cause.
It's the little things that light my way,
The simple moments in each day.

A laugh shared in the darkest hour,
A smile that blooms like a hidden flower.
A quiet "thank you" softly spoken,
A word that heals when hearts are broken.

It's in the small things, pure and true,
That I find strength to make it through.
A kind gesture, a glance of hope,
A tiny spark that helps me cope.

In every smile, I see the grace
Of why I'm here, in this tough place.
Each laugh is like a breath of air,
A reminder that someone cares.

The "thank yous" whispered from the heart,
Are the moments that set me apart.
They fill the gaps where fear once grew,
And help me face what I must do.

It's the little things that keep me strong,
The bits of joy that carry me along.
For in this work, so rough and vast,
It's the smallest moments that truly last.

**I Miss the Moments at Home,
but I Know I'm Protecting Them**

I miss the moments at home, it's true,
The simple things, the laughter too.
The quiet dinners, the warm embrace,
The love I see in each familiar face.

I miss the mornings, the sunrise glow,
The gentle moments when time moves slow.
The stories told, the smiles shared,
The comfort of knowing that someone cared.

But here I stand, so far away,
Protecting them, day by day.
For every step I take in stride,
I keep them safe on the other side.

I miss the moments, the life I knew,
But in my heart, I see the view
Of why I serve, of why I stand,
To guard my home, my precious land.

Each day apart, each night alone,
I carry with me thoughts of home.
But I know this duty, strong and true,
Is what I do for all of you.

I miss the moments, yes, I do,
But I protect the life we'll come back to.
And that's the reason I march ahead,
For home, for love, for what's unsaid.

The Bond with My Comrades
Is Stronger Than Words Can Say

The bond with my comrades, forged in fire,
Is stronger than words can ever inspire.
In the silence of battle, in moments of fear,
Their presence beside me is crystal clear.

We've walked through the darkest of nights, hand in
hand,
Faced down the storms in this foreign land.
No need for speeches, no need for praise,
The strength we share is a silent blaze.

In every glance, in every nod,
We know the weight of this shared facade.
The struggles we carry, the things we've seen,
The battles fought in places between.

No words can capture the trust we build,
The courage that rises when blood is spilled.
It's a bond unbroken, forged in strain,
Through loss and victory, through joy and pain.

We stand as one, in the fiercest fight,
Guided by honor, by shared light.
For in their eyes, I see my own,
A brotherhood deeper than I've ever known.

It's stronger than words could ever convey,
A bond that won't fade or drift away.
With my comrades, I know I'm strong,
Together we stand, where we belong.

In moments of triumph, in times of despair,
I know my comrades will always be there.
For the bond we share, no words can express—
It's a strength, a love, that's truly endless.

Every Scar Tells a Story, but Not All of Them Are Visible

Every scar upon my skin,
Tells a tale of where I've been.
A battle fought, a trial passed,
A moment carved that seems to last.

But not all scars are plain to see,
Some live deep inside of me.
The wounds that words can never show,
The quiet pain that few will know.

The ones that hide behind my eyes,
Where memories of dark times lie.
They shape my heart, they pull me tight,
They haunt my thoughts through sleepless nights.

For every scar the world can trace,
There's another time, another place
Where battles raged within my mind,
And left a mark that's hard to find.

The outside heals, the bruises fade,
But in my soul, the scars are laid.
Each one a story, sharp and clear,
Of fear and loss, of love and cheer.

Some scars are worn with pride and grace,
A reminder of the wars we face.
But many more are hidden deep,
The silent ones that never sleep.

So, when you see a scar I show,
Know there's more you'll never know.
For every mark upon my skin,
There's a story buried deep within.

I Don't Wear a Cape,
but I Do What I Can to Save the Day

I don't wear a cape, no mask or flight,
But I still stand in the darkest night.
I don't have powers, no super speed,
But I answer every call, every need.

I rise when the world is falling apart,
With steady hands and a willing heart.
I don't fly high, but I stand my ground,
In places where no heroes are found.

I fight the fires, I calm the storm,
I offer hope when fear is born.
For every life, for every plea,
I give my all, relentlessly.

I don't wear a cape, but I'm always there,
In moments of chaos, I show I care.
I run to the danger, I face the unknown,
Doing what I can, never alone.

It's not for fame, not for the praise,
But for the lives I strive to raise.
No cape, no mask, no magic to show,
Just heart and grit, wherever I go.

I may not soar or stop a train,
But I help ease another's pain.
In simple acts, in steady hands,
I save the day in ways I can.

So, though I don't wear a hero's cape,
I face the fight, I don't escape.
I may be small in the grand display,
But I do what I can to save the day.

The Sound of Footsteps Returning, Finally

The sound of footsteps on the floor,
A distant echo by the door.
At first, I wonder could it be?
Then joy erupts inside of me.

They're coming home, the wait is done,
The battles fought, the war is won.
The silence fades, the door swings wide,
And there they stand, with love and pride.

The sound of footsteps, strong and clear,
The sweetest music I'll ever hear.
A heart that raced for months on end
Now fills with peace, as they ascend.

Laughter rises, hugs so tight,
Faces glowing in the light.
Tears of joy that softly stream,
The homecoming we've dared to dream.

The bags are heavy, the boots worn down,
But none of that can steal the crown
The crown of love that waits within,
For those who've fought and now begin.

The sound of footsteps, steady, sure,
No need to wait or fear no more.
They've come back home, where they belong,
Where love is deep, and hope is strong.

So let the echoes fill the air,
With joy that only few compare.
For in those steps, our hearts revive
The sound of home, the sound of life.

The Legacy of Service Passed Down

The legacy of service, passed down through time,
From father to daughter, from mother to son's line.
A torch that's carried, a flame that burns bright,
Guiding each generation through the darkest night.

In whispered stories and medals worn,
In quiet strength that was never born
From pride or glory, but from hearts so true,
The legacy of service carries through.

I watched my parents stand so tall,
Answering the call when duty called.
With every step, with every task,
They taught me that service was never too much to
ask.

It's in the hands that build and heal,
The courage to face the turning wheel.
It's in the moments where fear is strong,
And the will to serve still carries on.

This legacy isn't etched in stone,
But in the lives that we have known.
In every flag, in every name,
It's passed along, a burning flame.

Now it's my turn to take the lead,
To serve with honor, to meet the need.
For the legacy runs in my veins,
A bond of service that forever remains.

It's passed through hearts, from old to new,
In every act, in all we do.
The legacy of service, strong and pure,
A gift that time will always endure.

The First American Flag

On a rainy September night so long ago,
The British ships sent fire below.
Shells and rockets, a storm of might,
Pounding Fort McHenry through the night.

For twenty-five hours, the battle raged,
As Baltimore Harbor's fate was staged.
A downpour of fury, relentless and loud,
Casting flames through smoke and cloud.

Weeks before, D.C. had burned,
The Capitol and White House overturned.
But here at McHenry, they stood their ground,
As shot and shell crashed all around.

In the distance, Francis Scott Key stood,
A lawyer, a patriot, watching as he could.
Eight miles away, he saw the sky,
Red bursts of fire as the hours crept by.

He feared defeat, the dawn would bring
The British flag, their anthem's ring.
But as the smoke began to part,
A sight of hope stirred in his heart.

At "the dawn's early light" it flew,
The American flag, bold and true.
Not the Union Jack, but stripes and stars,
Proclaiming victory from the scars.

Key's hand moved quickly, capturing grace,
The triumph found in that hallowed place.
His words would soon become a song,
A nation's pride where they belong.

"The Star-Spangled Banner" rose from the fight,
Born of that dark, victorious night.
A symbol now, for all to see,
Of a young nation's bravery.

The flag still lives, though worn by years,
Tattered, but held in reverent cheers.
An emblem of freedom, courage, and pride,
A story that time cannot hide.

In battle's storm, it stood so high,
A beacon of hope against the sky.
The first American flag that flew
Still reminds us of what is true.

Through fire, fear, and cannon's roar,
The flag endured, forever more.
A testament to the spirit bold,
Of a land whose story is yet to be told.

Oh Beautiful for Gracious Skies

Oh beautiful for gracious skies,
Where amber waves of grain arise,
This land of promise, wide and free,
A gift of grace for you and me.

From mountain peaks to rolling plains,
Across the rivers, through the rains,
We walk in freedom, side by side,
In this great nation, filled with pride.

For every field, for every shore,
We hold a blessing at our core.
A land of hope, a land of dreams,
Where nothing is as far as it seems.

The amber waves that gently sway,
Remind us of each precious day
A place to live, a place to grow,
With boundless skies, where freedoms flow.

The gracious skies, the fertile ground,
Are gifts that in our hearts resound.
For we are blessed to call this home,
To claim the earth beneath our roam.

Oh beautiful, this land of grace,
Where every creed and every face
Finds a home, a voice, a place to stand,
In the heart of this free, united land.

And as we gaze on skies so high,
We thank the stars, the stripes that fly.
For we are blessed, it's plain to see—
This land was made for you and me.

A Moment of Silence Before the Storm

A moment of silence, still and deep,
As the world holds its breath, and the shadows creep.
The air is heavy, the sky turns gray,
Waiting for the storm to have its say.

No winds yet howl, no thunder roars,
But something stirs on distant shores.
In this quiet, a calm unknown,
A fleeting peace before it's blown.

Hearts beat faster, eyes look wide,
For in this hush, we cannot hide.
The storm will come, with all its might,
But for now, there's only quiet light.

A moment to breathe, a chance to pause,
Before the chaos shakes its claws.
To gather strength, to stand so strong,
For storms don't last, but they come on long.

In the silence, we find our will,
A promise to fight, to stand up still.
For after the storm, the skies will clear,
But in this moment, we face our fear.

A moment of silence before the fray,
Before the storm takes light away.
Yet in the quiet, our hope is born
Ready to face what comes with the dawn.

The Warrior's Heart, Never Truly at Rest

The warrior's heart, though battle is done,
Never truly rests beneath the sun.
The fight may fade, the field may clear,
But echoes of war are always near.

In the silence of night, the mind still roams,
To distant lands, to broken homes.
Though the hands are still, the spirit stirs,
Remembering battles, sights, and slurs.

Each scar, each memory, a part of the soul,
A warrior's life that's never whole.
For even in peace, the heart beats fast,
Haunted by shadows of the past.

The warrior stands, but never free,
From the weight of what once had to be.
For courage comes at a quiet cost,
Of sleepless nights and moments lost.

Yet still they rise, with strength anew,
Carrying burdens the world never knew.
For though the battle's laid to rest,
The warrior's heart will never rest.

Always ready, always on guard,
The wounds within, forever scarred.
A heart that beats with love and pain
The warrior's legacy will remain.

I Live Near Camp Pendleton, With Marines All Around

I live near Camp Pendleton, Marines all around,
I may not fight, but here in my town,
I do what I can, in my own simple way,
To show them respect, to brighten their day.

My door is always open wide,
For anyone in uniform to step inside.
To sit, share a meal, feel at ease,
Surrounded by family, with warmth like a breeze.

Here, they are welcome, a place they can rest,
For now, this is home, and I'll give my best.
I've never let a Marine pay for his meal,
For in my home, it's gratitude that's real.

So, look around, find your way too,
To show the servicemen your gratitude true.
There should never be a hero sitting alone,
No empty seat for those far from home.

Thanksgiving's warm, with turkey and grace,
Christmas with gifts and an open space.
Our home's a shelter from the miles they roam,
For any Marine, this is their home.

From turkey breast to a welcoming smile,
We'll share with them for just a while.
I may not fight, but in my own way,
I honor their service, day by day.

The Quiet Tears of a Soldier

The quiet tears of a soldier fall,
Where no one sees, no one calls.
In the silence of the night so still,
Where courage battles against the will.

The world sees strength, the world sees pride,
But deep within, emotions hide.
For even the bravest have their fears,
And every warrior sheds their tears.

They've stood in the fire, faced the fight,
But in the dark, when there's no light,
The weight of war, the cost of pain,
Creeps in, like a haunting rain.

They cry not for glory lost or won,
But for the souls, for what's undone.
For brothers and sisters who didn't return,
For the memories that forever burn.

Each tear is quiet, no sound is made,
A soldier's grief, silently laid.
For though their strength can never break,
The quiet tears, their toll they take.

But in those tears, there's honor too,
A heart that feels what they've been through.
For the bravest souls still bleed inside,
In the quiet, where their truths reside.

The quiet tears of a soldier fall,
A testament to giving their all.
They wipe them away, then rise again
A silent hero, with pain to mend.

The Oath Sworn to Protect, at Any Cost

The oath is sworn, the promise made,
To stand for those who are afraid.
To guard, defend, and bear the weight,
Of duty's call, of freedom's fate.

At any cost, no matter when,
The oath is carried by women and men.
Through fire, through storm, through darkest night,
They hold the line, they face the fight.

It's not for glory, nor for gain,
But for the peace others sustain.
For every life they choose to save,
They walk the path the brave must pave.

At any cost, through trials vast,
They honor the flag, they hold it fast.
For in their heart, a fire ignites
A vow to rise for others' rights.

The oath sworn strong, no turning back,
Through skies of blue or fields of black.
They stand as shields, no matter the cost,
For freedom won, for lives not lost.

The weight is heavy, the road is long,
But the oath they swear makes them strong.
To protect, to serve, without a pause,
They carry the burden of the cause.

At any cost, they will defend,
Until their mission finds its end.
For the oath is more than words they speak
It's a promise they vow to forever keep.

The Soldier's Dreams of Peace, Elusive

The soldier dreams of peace, but finds it far,
A flicker fading like a distant star.
Elusive, slipping from his grasp,
Each time he reaches, it won't last.

In quiet moments, when battles cease,
He longs for silence, longs for peace.
But even in the calmest night,
Old memories come back to bite.

The echoes of war still fill his mind,
No rest, no peace for him to find.
The dreams of safety, joy, and light
Fade into the shadows of the fight.

He dreams of peace, of days serene,
Of meadows soft and skies of green.
But in his heart, the war still roars,
A raging storm behind closed doors.

For peace is something just out of view,
A dream too distant, though overdue.
He reaches for it, in his sleep,
But war's dark scars run far too deep.

The soldier's dreams of peace remain,
Elusive, slipping through his pain.
Yet still he hopes, and still he prays,
That peace will come one of these days.

The War That Did Not End

He comes home with a smile, a hero's grace,
But deep inside, he's in another place.
The battles fought, the wars he braved,
Are scars that time has never saved.

At night, he wakes with a startled scream,
Caught in the grip of a haunting dream.
Flashbacks blur the lines of time,
The war still rages in his mind.

The bed becomes a battlefield,
The darkness holds no shield.
He fights the ghosts, he fights the fear,
Not wanting to let his family near.

They don't know the fight he sees,
The moments that drop him to his knees.
For them, the war is long since past,
But for him, the shadows cast.

He calms his breath, he hides his pain,
So they won't feel his hurt again.
For though he's home, the truth remains
The war inside him never wanes.

He loves them more than words can say,
But he's afraid they'll turn away.
So, he fights the battle on his own,
In the quiet hours, all alone.

Each morning, he puts on a brave face,
Hoping one day to find his place.
But deep within, the struggle stays
For him, the war did not end with praise.

So, when you see him standing tall,
Remember the battles that still call.
For though he's home, the fight's not through,
And every night, the war renews.

The Wings of an Angel Carrying a Fallen Hero

The wings of an angel, soft and wide,
Carry a hero to the other side.
A soldier fallen, brave and true,
Now lifted high through skies of blue.

In silence, the angel gently flies,
With tearful whispers and heavy skies.
The weight of a life, the cost of war,
Held by wings forevermore.

No words are spoken, none need to be,
For the angel knows the pain we see.
The sacrifice, the life they gave,
Now cradled gently in heaven's wave.

The fallen hero, at last in peace,
Their battles end, their suffering cease.
Carried home, to rest and heal,
In wings of light, their fate is sealed.

The angel's wings, so strong, so kind,
Take the hero, leave none behind.
And in the sky, a tear does fall,
For a hero answered their final call.

Now in the arms of angels bright,
The fallen hero soars through light.
Their courage honored, their story told,
As wings of an angel, pure as gold.

They fly beyond, no more to roam,
Carried by wings that guide them home.
A fallen hero, forever free,
Held by an angel's eternity.

The Honor Guard's Solemn Salute

The honor guard stands straight and tall,
In silent rows, they heed the call.
Their faces set, their hearts are true,
Draped in red, white, and blue.

The air is thick, the world holds still,
As they prepare with iron will.
Their rifles raised, their voices mute,
For this, the honor guard's salute.

With every step, with every stance,
They honor one who took the chance.
A soldier's journey now complete,
Laid to rest with quiet feet.

The bugle plays its mournful song,
A farewell note, so pure, so long.
And as the flag is folded tight,
They stand as guardians of the light.

A final shot, a measured cry,
A tear falls from the watching eye.
For this salute, in quiet grace,
Is given for the fallen's place.

No words are spoken, none are said,
But in their silence, honor's led.
A hero gone, but not forgot,
Held by those who gave a lot.

The honor guard, with heads bowed low,
Salutes the brave they've come to know.
In every step, in every glance,
They stand for freedom's lasting chance.

The solemn salute, the rifles raised,
A tribute to the life they praised.
For in this still and sacred ground,
The honor guard stands all around.

The Heartbeat of a Nation in a Soldier's Chest

The heartbeat of a nation strong,
Beats in a soldier all along.
In every step, in every breath,
They carry freedom, life, and death.

With every pulse that fills their veins,
The weight of history remains.
The flag they fight for, bold and true,
In every heartbeat echoes through.

In fields of battle, near and far,
Their hearts become our guiding star.
The heartbeat of a nation's pride,
Is carried in the steps they stride.

They wear the hopes of those they serve,
In every battle, every nerve.
The dreams of peace, the fight for right,
Held in their chest through darkest night.

And though they march, through storm or flame,
They bear the pulse of freedom's name.
A soldier's heart, a nation's guide,
With every beat, we stand beside.

For in their chest, our stories live,
The sacrifice they freely give.
The heartbeat of a land so free,
In every soldier's chest will be.

So, when they fight, they fight for all,
With every rise, with every fall.
The heartbeat of a nation blessed,
Beats forever in a soldier's chest.

Hello, I'm Believe Lylyianne every sale/donation of a book, helps supply angel sessions for victims of domestic violence, human trafficing and to support our military adjust back into their family lives once they are home. I've been a therapist and hypnotherapist for over 35 years. I have a system that is fast and effective at helping people. My clients constantly tell me that I've helpe them over come trauma in 4 months that 20 years of therapy did not acheive. I have never turned anyone away that needed help. Your donations and purchases goes into a fund as angel sessions. I also do alot of public speaking on energy and how to not fall pray to situations that can become deadly. Please Join Me In this Fight. I am always filled withe gratitude for every dollar we have to help someone.

Always with Light and Love,
Believe

Visit our website to find other Merchandise and Books
to Help Save Our Youth
BelieveLylyianne.com
Believe.guru

Made in the USA
Columbia, SC
05 October 2024

43120735R00104